How to Draw Rockets

Step-by-Step Guide

Best Rocket Drawing Book for You and Your Kids

BY

ANDY HOPPER

Copyright Notes

Table of Contents

Introduction

Kids have this intense desire to express themselves the ways they know how to. During their formative years, drawing all sorts is on top of their favorite things to do. You ought to encourage as it boosts their creativity and generally advances their cognitive development.

This book is written to give you and your kids the smoothest drawing experience with the different guides and instructions on how to draw different kinds of objects and animals. However, you should note that drawing, like everything worthwhile, requires a great deal of patience and consistency. Be patient with your kids as they wade through the tips and techniques in this book and put them into practice. Now, they will not get everything on the first try, but do not let this deter them. Be by their side at every step of the way and gently encourage them. In no time, they will be perfect little creators, and you, their trainer.

Besides, this is a rewarding activity to do as it presents you the opportunity of hanging out with your kids and connecting with them in ways you never knew was possible. The book contains all the help you need, now sit down with them and help them do this.

That is pretty much all about it - we should start this exciting journey now, shouldn't we?

How to draw Rocket 1

Step 1.

Draw a narrow elongated body with sharp ends.

Step 2.

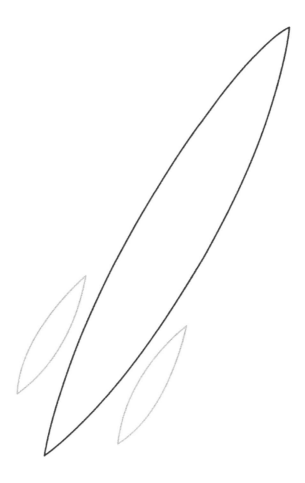

Add alongside two more similar cases but less.

Step 3.

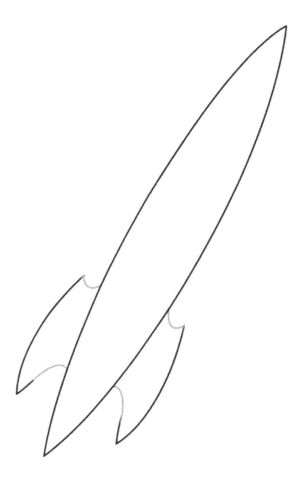

Remove unnecessary lines and connect smaller elements with a large body with four curved lines.

Step 4.

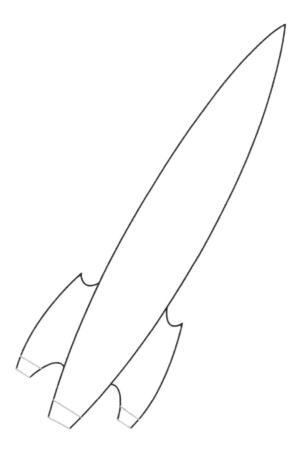

Add strips to the bottom of all elements and remove sharp
ends.

Step 5.

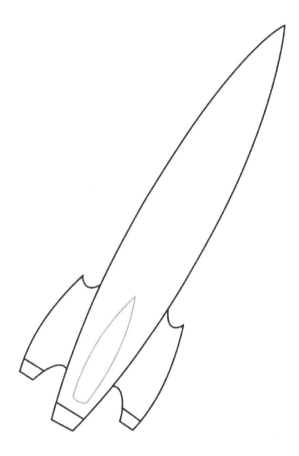

Add another small element similar in shape to a large copy.

Step 6.

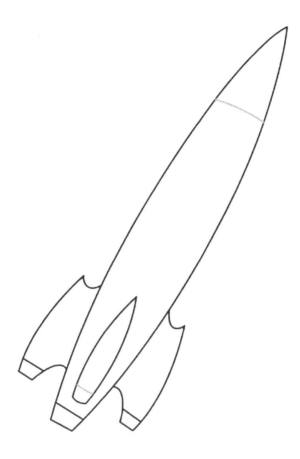

Add a line at the bottom of the previous figure and on the nose of the rocket.

Step 7.

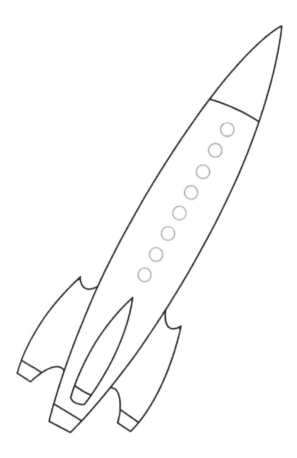

Draw portholes along a large rocket hull.

Step 8.

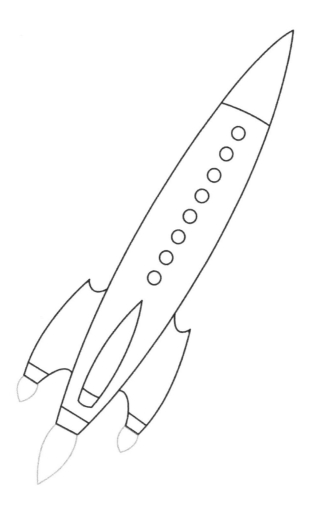

Draw a fire from the engines.

Step 9.

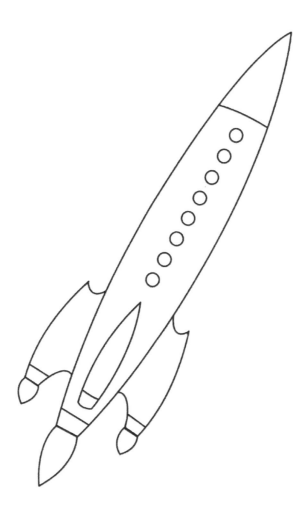

Done, let's start coloring!

Step 10.

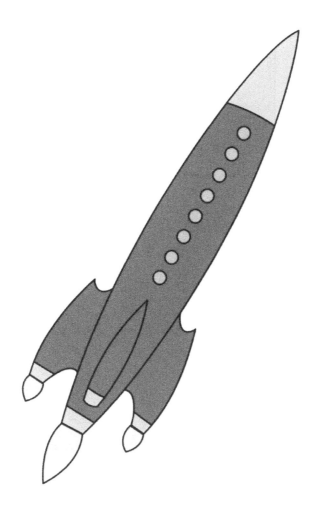

Color picture using red, grey and blue.

Step 11.

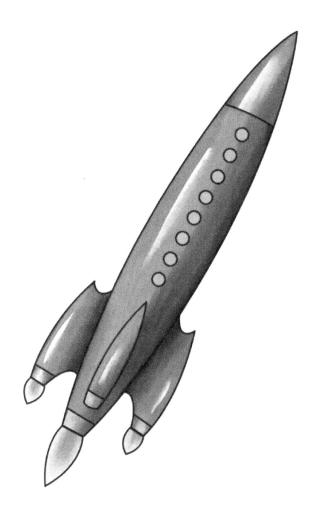

Add some shadows and highlights to add volume.

Step 12.

Colored version.

How to draw Rocket 2

Step 1.

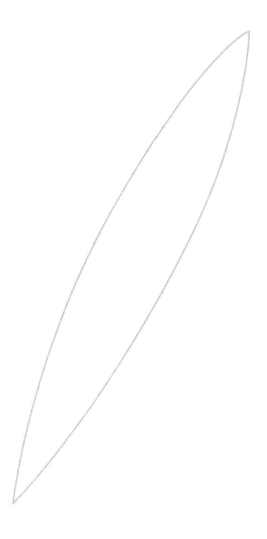

Draw a narrow elongated body with sharp ends.

Step 2.

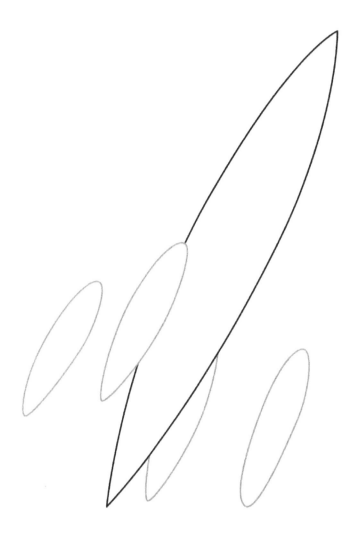

Add alongside four more similar cases but less.

Step 3.

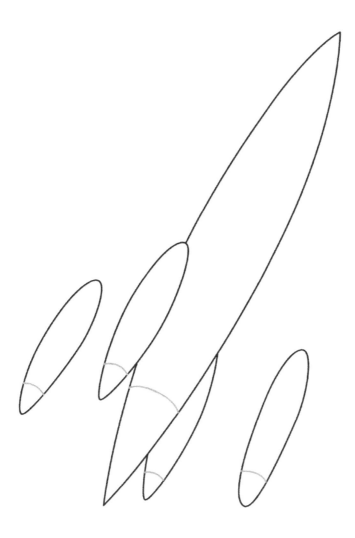

Add strips to all parts of the rocket as shown in the example.

Step 4.

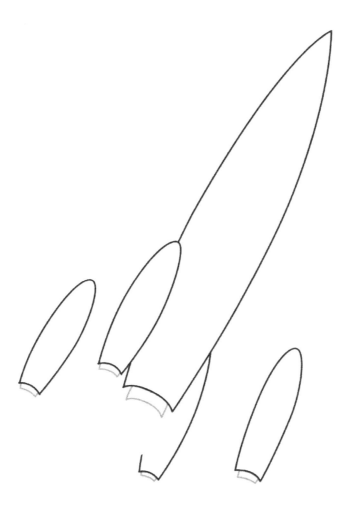

Remove the bottom of all the elements and draw one rectangle under each.

Step 5.

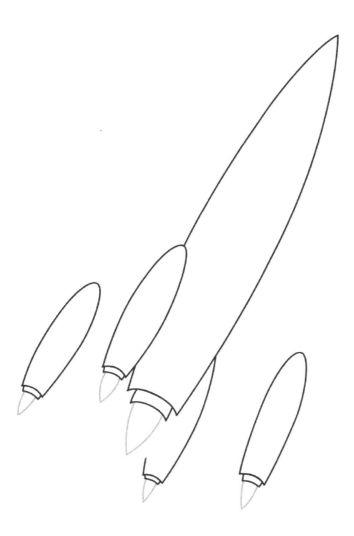

Draw a sharp fire from all engines.

Step 6.

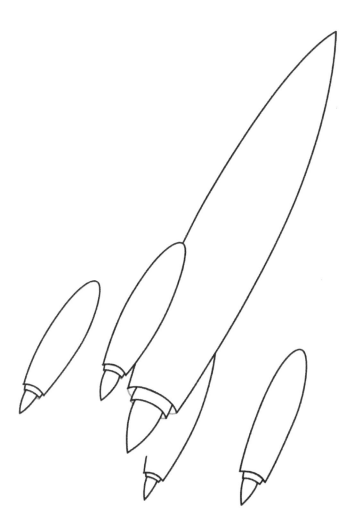

Add a few lines as shown on the original.

Step 7.

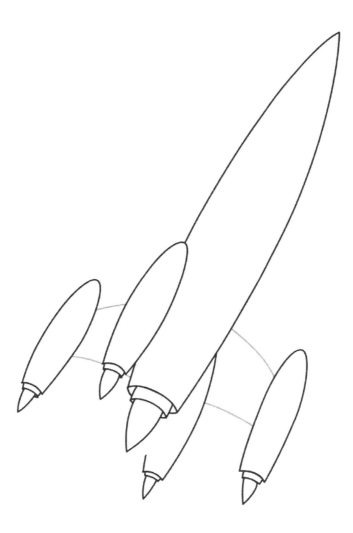

Connect all parts of the rocket with four curved lines.

Step 8.

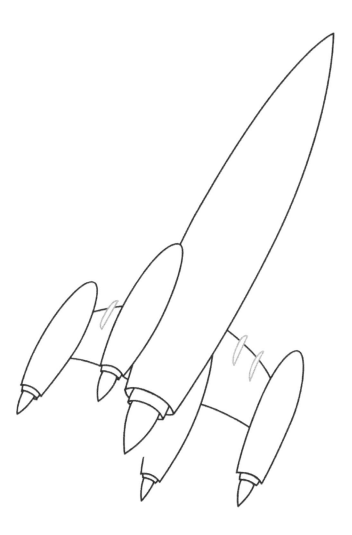

Add a few elements to the connections.

Step 9.

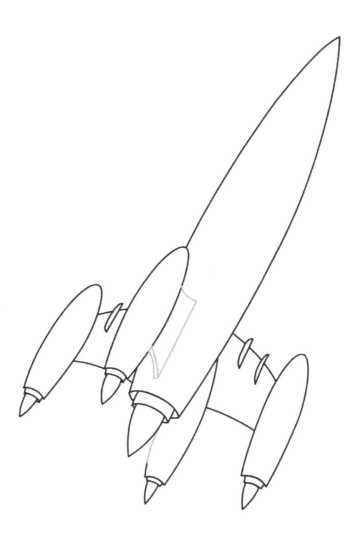

Add a connection between the front and the main.

Step 10.

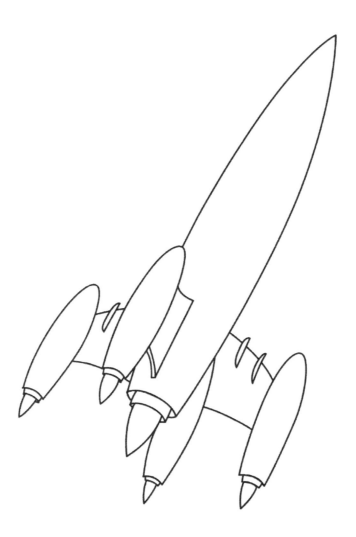

Done, let's start coloring!

Step 11.

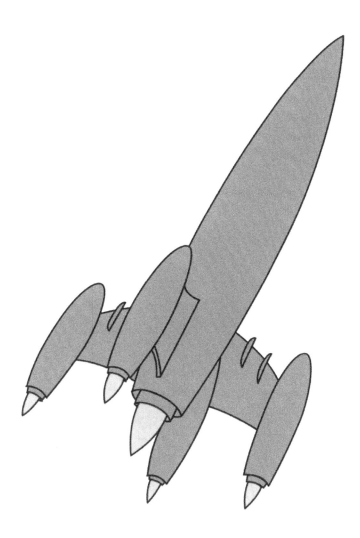

Color picture using grey and blue.

Step 12.

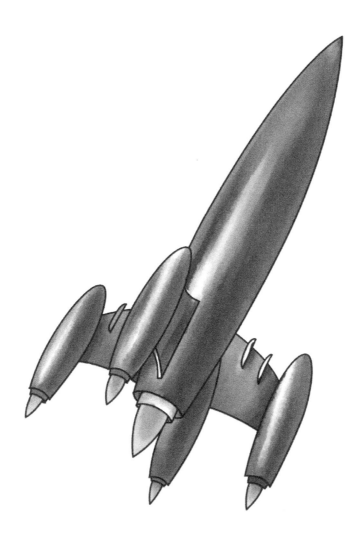

Add some shadows and highlights to add volume.

Step 13.

Colored version.

How to draw Rocket 3

Step 1.

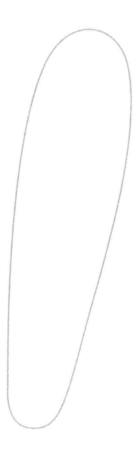

Draw a large elongated oval, as shown in the example.

Step 2.

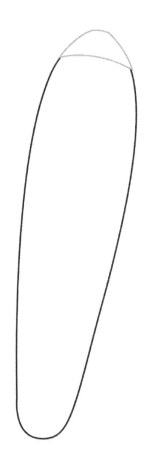

Draw a rocket nose.

Step 3.

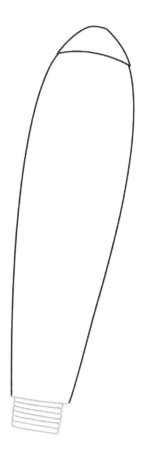

Draw a rocket engine.

Step 4.

Add an antenna to the rocket nose.

Step 5.

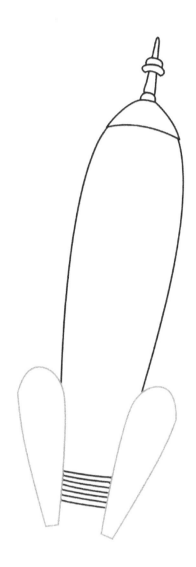

Add two elongated ovals on the left and right sides.

Step 6.

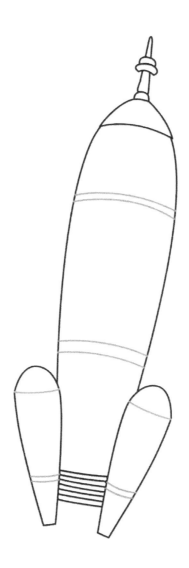

Add lines to the whole area of the rocket.

Step 7.

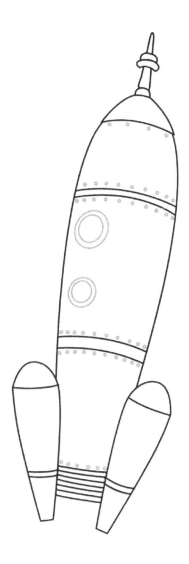

Draw two portholes and bolts along the lines on the rocket.

Step 8.

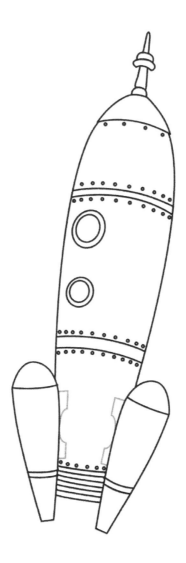

Arise connecting fastenings between the big case and two small ones.

Step 9.

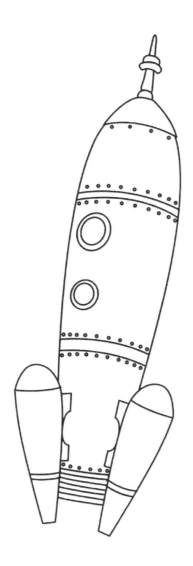

Done, let's start coloring!

Step 10.

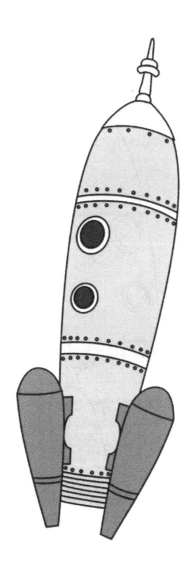

Color picture using blue, grey and red.

Step 11.

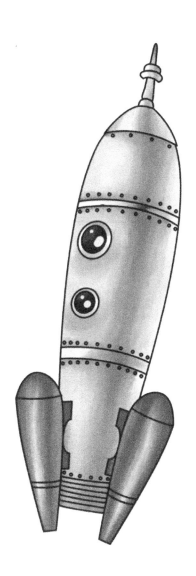

Add some shadows and highlights to add volume.

Step 12.

Colored version.

How to draw Rocket 4

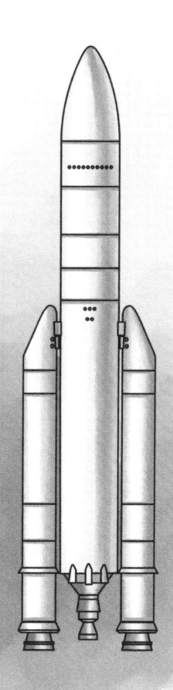

Step 1.

Draw a long rocket body in the form of a rectangle with a triangular top.

Step 2.

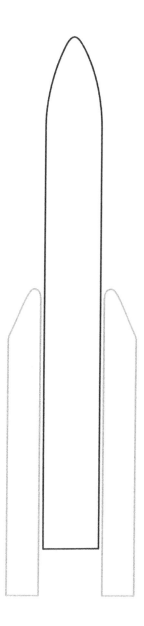

Add on the left and right side another 2 smaller bodies.

Step 3.

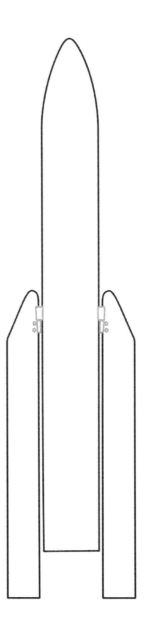

Add connections between large and small enclosures.

Step 4.

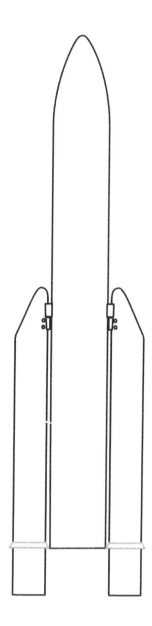

Add two rectangles to the bottom of two small enclosures.

Step 5.

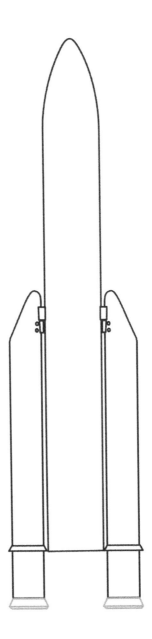

Add two engines at the bottom.

Step 6.

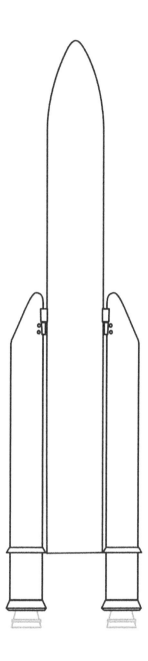

Add lines to the main body and some details at the bottom.

Step 7.

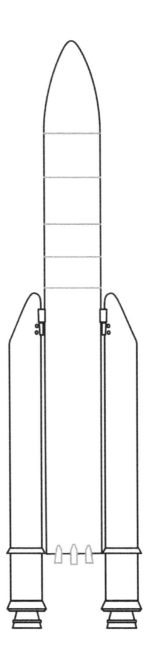

Add parts at the bottom of the large case.

Step 8.

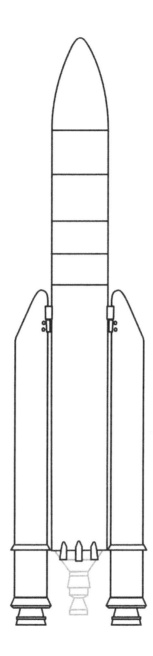

Add engines to the bottom of the large case.

Step 9.

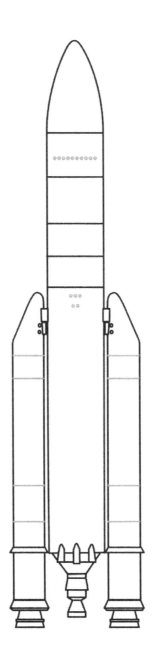

Add lines across the entire rocket.

Step 10.

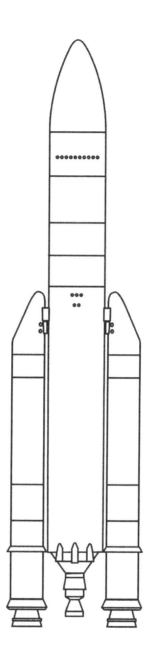

Done, let's start coloring!

Step 11.

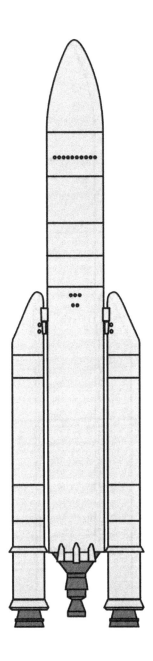

Color picture using beige.

Step 12.

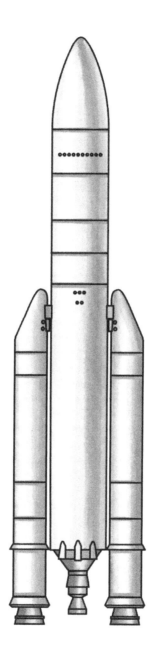

Add some shadows and highlights to add volume.

Step 13.

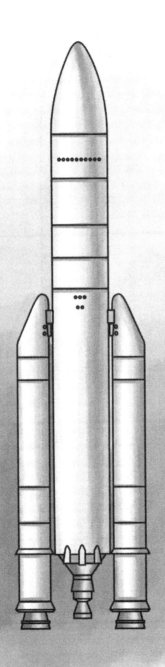

Colored version.

How to draw Rocket 5

Step 1.

Draw the rocket body as shown in the example.

Step 2.

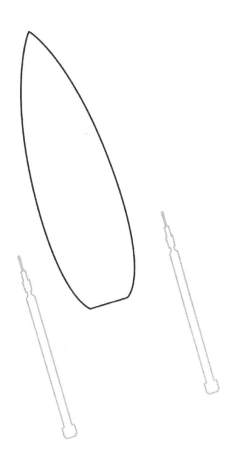

Draw two sharp details on both sides of the case.

Step 3.

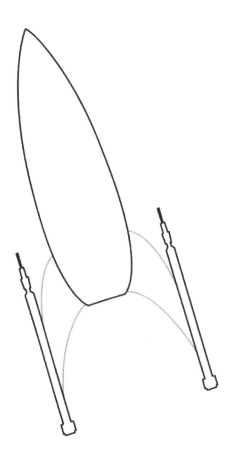

Connect the body and sharp parts with four curved lines.

Step 4.

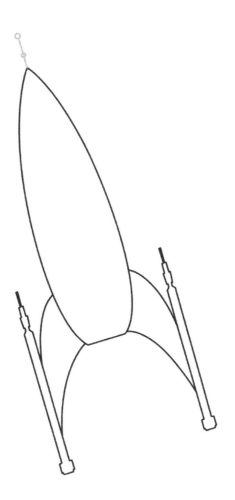

Add an antenna to the nose.

Step 5.

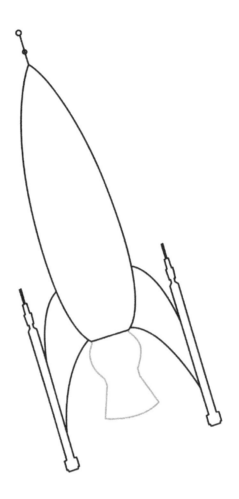

Draw a rocket engine, be close to the original.

Step 6.

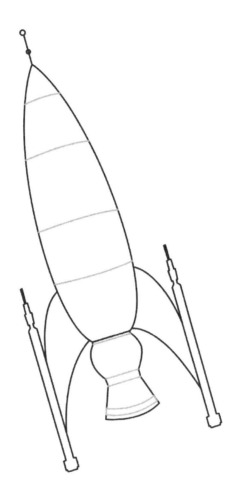

Add lines to the rocket body for decoration.

Step 7.

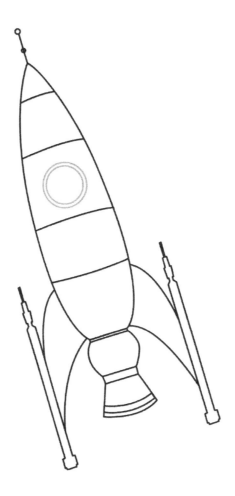

Add a porthole to the case.

Step 8.

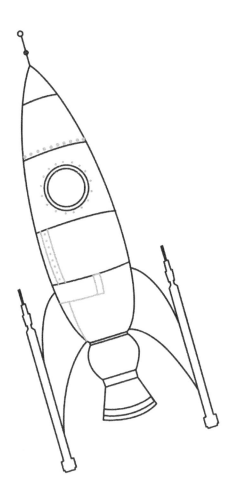

Add lines as shown in the example.

Step 9.

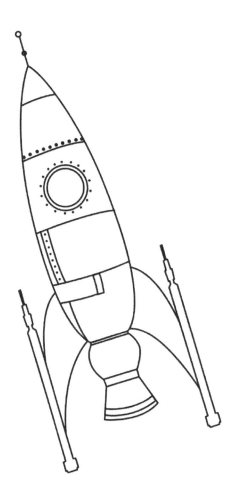

Done, let's start coloring!

Step 10.

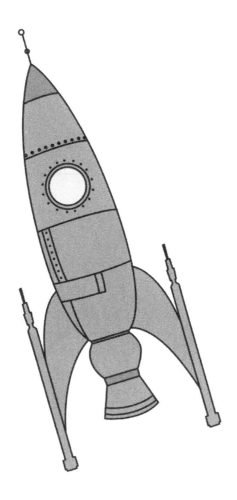

Color picture using grey, red and blue.

Step 11.

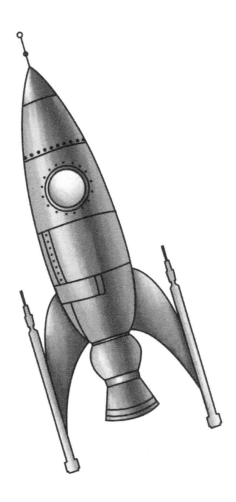

Add some shadows and highlights to add volume.

Step 12.

Colored version.

How to draw Rocket 6

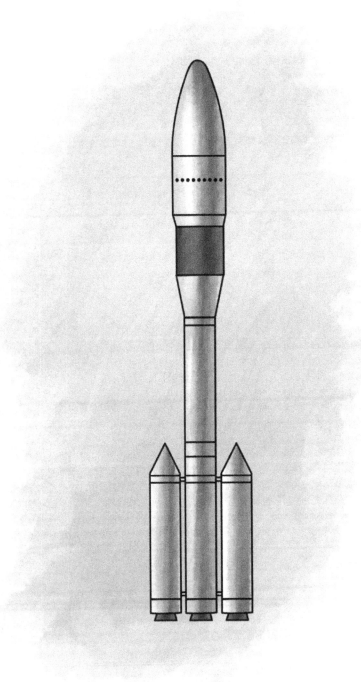

Step 1.

Draw the upper part of the rocket in the upper part of the sheet.

Step 2.

Add a small detail under the first figure.

Step 3.

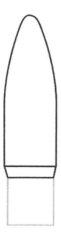

Draw a rectangle just below.

Step 4.

Draw a small inverted trapezoid.

Step 5.

Draw a long rectangle.

Step 6.

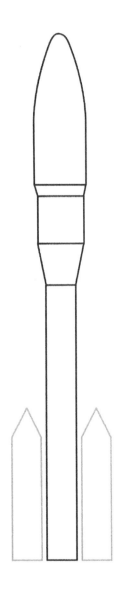

Draw two middle rectangles with a triangular top.

Step 7.

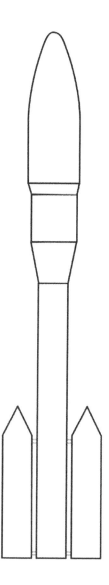

Draw several lines to connect the details.

Step 8.

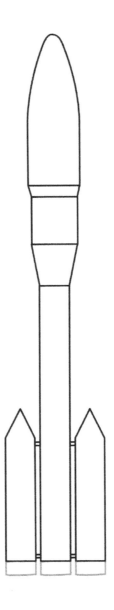

Draw small rectangles at the bottom of three parts.

Step 9.

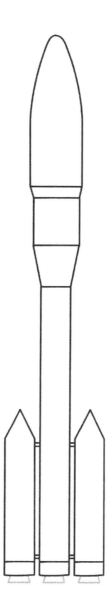

Draw small trapezium for engines.

Step 10.

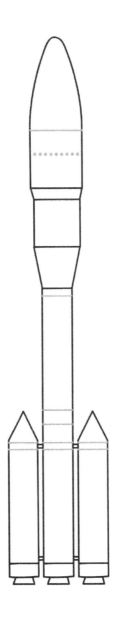

Add details by drawing lines to the body of the rocket.

Step 11.

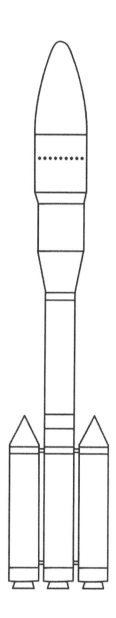

Done, let's start coloring!

Step 12.

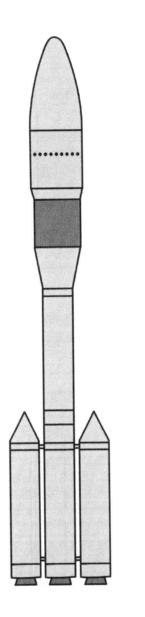

Color picture using grey.

Step 13.

Add some shadows and highlights to add volume.

Step 14.

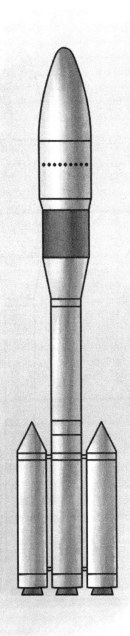

Colored version.

How to draw Rocket 7

Step 1.

Draw the upper part of the rocket in the upper part of the sheet.

Step 2.

Add a small detail under the first figure.

Step 3.

Draw a rectangle just below.

Step 4.

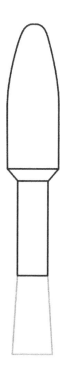

Draw a small trapezoid.

Step 5.

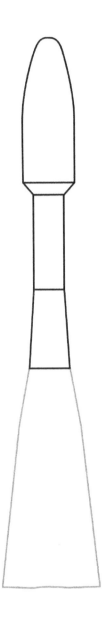

Draw another trapezium lower larger.

Step 6.

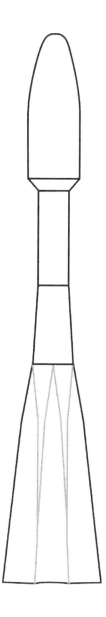

Add four curved lines that connect in two.

Step 7.

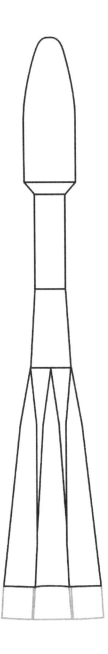

Draw three more rectangles below.

Step 8.

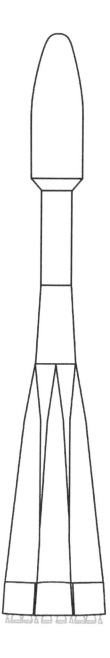

Add engines below.

Step 9.

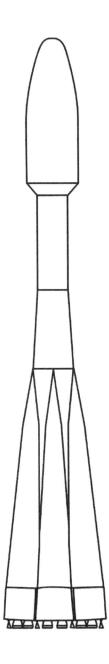

Done, let's start coloring!

Step 10.

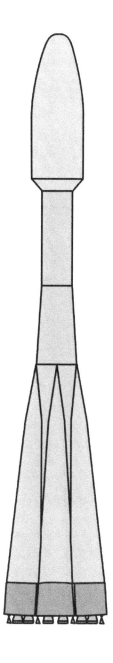

Color picture using grey, green and orange.

Step 11.

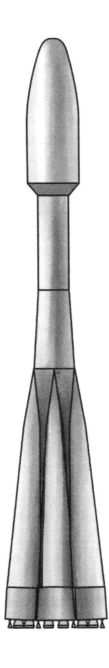

Add some shadows and highlights to add volume.

Step 12.

Colored version.

About the Author

Andy Hopper is an American illustrator born in sunny California just a hair's breadth from the beautiful Sierra foothills. After studying Design and Media at UCLA, Andy decided to try his hand at teaching his own unique style of art to novice artists just starting out with their craft.

He has won numerous art awards and has several publications in print and e-book to his credit. His e-books teach the beginner artist how to draw using simple techniques suitable for all ages. While Andy prefers using chalk, pencil and pastels for his own artwork, but has been known to dabble in the world of watercolour from time to time and teach this skill to his students.

Andy Hopper lives just outside of Los Angeles in Santa Monica, California with his wife of 15 years and their three children. His art studio is a welcome respite to the area and he has been known to start impromptu outdoor art sessions with the people in his neighborhood for no charge.

Made in the USA
Monee, IL
21 December 2023

50301410R00057